50 WILDEST BIBLE STORIES

50 WILDEST BIBLE STORIES

Andy Robb

CWR

Intro

Congratulations!

Buying this book is one of the smartest decisions you'll ever make if you're wanting to get your teeth into the Bible but aren't quite sure where to start. Not only have we hand-picked some of the best bits for you, but we've also chopped them up into nice, easy-to-chomp morsels. How's that for thoughtfulness?

In this tasty book we've served up fifty juicy, bite-sized bits of the Bible to munch on and loads of crazy cartoon pics to make them easy for you to digest.

To keep you on your toes, we've mixed up the Old and New Testament stories. Not sure what the difference is between them? It's simple. New Testament stories kick off from when Jesus showed up on planet Earth. The Old Testament happened before that and goes right back to the beginning of time.

But if you're thinking that this

book is all about being spoon-fed stuff from the Bible so that you don't have to lift a finger, think again! At the end of each Bible bit there's some investigating work for you to do, which means you'll need to get your hands on a Bible if you want to find out how the stories end.

Just in case you've bought this book but you don't know much about the Bible, let me give you some useful facts …

Fact number one:

Although the Bible is one book (and what a whopper it is), it's actually made up of sixty-six mini books.

Fact number two:

The Bible wasn't written by just one person like most books. It has over forty authors.

Fact number three:

The Bible was written over a period of roughly 1,500 years.

Fact number four:

Everything that's in the Bible was God's idea.

Next up, you're gonna need to know how to read the Bible – and I don't mean from left to right and top to bottom.

The first thing to know is that every Bible book has got its own name, such as Joshua, Judges, Job, Jeremiah, Joel, Jonah,

John, James or Jude. To make these Bible books easier to read, they're handily divided up into chapters (like normal books) and then each chapter is broken up into verses (like you get in poems). All clear so far? Good!

So, if you wanted to check out Bible book Genesis, chapter 5 and verses 25 to 27, here's how it's often written down:

Genesis 5:25-27

Check out these verses and you'll discover who the world's oldest man was (ever) and how many birthday cards he would have received if they'd been invented way back then (which they hadn't).

That's about it.

So what are you waiting for? Tuck in!

SNAKES ALIVE!

I f you think that the tale of Doctor Dolittle is a bit far-fetched, try this wild Bible story (with talking animals) for size. The action takes place soon after God created the universe that we all live in.

God's finishing touch was a rather small (but very special) planet called Earth, which He filled with all sorts of weird and wonderful animals and lots of juicy vegetation for them to feed on.

Next up, God needed someone to make sure planet Earth was looked after the way He wanted, so God made a couple of human beings. No prizes for guessing that the world's first two people were none other than Adam and Eve. This perfect pair hung out in a place called the Garden of Eden, and they were free to munch on whatever yummy fruit grew there … with one exception. On no account whatsoever were they to eat from the tree of the knowledge of good and evil. God warned them that if they did, they'd die. Gulp!

Anyway, all was going well between Adam and Eve and God until a sly, slippery serpent slithered into the garden and began to sow seeds of doubt in Eve's mind about whether what God had said was actually true. Did God

really say they shouldn't eat the fruit from that tree? Would they really die? Surely not! Well, that's what the cunning (and talking) serpent suggested to her. Eve had a good old think about it and then decided that the fruit from the tree of the knowledge of good and evil looked far too scrummy to ignore. Throwing caution to the wind, she took a chomp of its juicy fruit. Deeeelicious! In fact, it was so nice she persuaded Adam to tuck in as well. Did they die? Well, not straight off, but they eventually did, which wasn't God's original plan for them.

That wasn't the only downside to Adam and Eve's disobedience. Up until then they'd been wandering around stark naked without so much as a blush. One munch of the forbidden fruit and the pair had suddenly lost their innocence. The Bible says that Adam and Eve knocked up some clothes out of fig leaves to cover their embarrassment.

God had one last bombshell to drop, but to find out what it is you'll have to head to Bible book Genesis, chapter 3 and read verses 20 to 24.

TOWER POWER

Most people have heard the story of Noah and his ark, that big, box-shaped boat which saved him, his family and a pair of every animal that lived on the face of the earth. Once the world's biggest flood had subsided, God told Noah and his family to have loads of kids and to fill the world with people again. So far so good. Over time the earth's population grew and grew and then, just when it looked like everything was going to plan, a bunch of them decided to put a spanner in the works.

Noah's descendants had been gradually heading away from where the ark had parked up (on Mount Ararat) in search of new land, but when they came to a flat bit of land in Babylonia, everyone downed luggage and came to an abrupt halt. They'd had enough of this living out of a suitcase lark. Time to settle down and build proper houses for themselves. Nothing wrong with that, you may think. Let's see what else they had to say for themselves. 'How about we build a whopping big tower that reaches up to heaven to show how great we are?' The thinking was that if they made a bit of a name for themselves, they'd be set up for life and could stay put in Babylonia. No more of

this 'filling the earth' stuff that God had told 'em to do. Who wants to keep moving around to new places when a comfortable life in Babylonia beckons?

God was having none of it. People who did as they pleased rather than obeying Him was the reason why He'd wiped them off the face of the earth in the first place. God had to do something before the rot set in again. Up until that point in history, everybody spoke the same language, but not for long. While the settlers were busy building their tower, God came down and put an end to their nonsense in an instant.

Check out what God did in Bible book Genesis, chapter 11 and verses 7 to 9.

PAST-IT PAIR

The clock was ticking for Abraham and his wife Sarah. The good news was that God had promised them a son and that they'd have so many descendants you wouldn't be able to count them on the fingers of a million hands (or words to that effect). The bad news was that Abraham and Sarah were getting on a bit. In fact, they were older than most of your grandparents, so things weren't looking too good. The past-it pair were now beginning to doubt whether God could really come through for them. Perhaps if they gave Him a bit of a helping hand … Sarah had the bright idea of Abraham having a kid by her servant girl (Hagar). In those days you could claim the baby as your own even if you hadn't given birth to it yourself.

So, that's what happened. But Sarah soon regretted her decision and things quickly turned sour between her and Hagar. Abraham wasn't about to get involved in a row between the two women and told Sarah to feel free to sort it out however she wanted. Sarah resented Hagar and made her life such a misery that the servant girl did a runner. Hagar fled into the desert where an angel of God caught up with her and asked what was up. After hearing Hagar's sorry tale he told her to go back to Sarah. God would look after Hagar and her baby (Ishmael) and because Abraham was the father, she'd also have so many descendants you couldn't count them.

To discover what sort of boy Ishmael turned out to be, you'll need to read Bible book Genesis, chapter 16 and verse 12.

BABY BATTLE

Jacob was a guy from the Bible who'd been hoping to marry a gal called Rachel but ended up getting hitched to her older sister Leah instead. Don't feel too sorry for Jacob because he did eventually get to marry the love of his life (Rachel) as well. Jacob was a bit miffed that he'd been landed with Leah and gave her the cold shoulder. God felt sorry for Leah and tried to cheer her up by giving her kids. First to be born was Reuben, followed by Simeon, Levi and Judah.

Meanwhile, Rachel was getting well cheesed off with Jacob for not having any kids with her. In desperation, Rachel gave Jacob her maidservant Bilhah to have a baby by, which he did. Two babies, to be precise. Dan and Naphtali.

So the score so far was Leah four, Rachel two. Leah wasn't gonna lose her lead and so gave Jacob her maidservant Zilpah for him to have kids by, which he did. Zilpah delivered a couple more boys called Gad and Asher.

Leah was on a bit of a roll and wasted no time in having two more boys herself (Issachar and Zebulun), and just to rub salt into the wound for Rachel, Leah also gave birth to a girl (Dinah). With the score now at 9–2 things weren't looking too good for Rachel and then, out of the blue, she went and had a boy. He was called Joseph and he's got a story all of his own to tell.

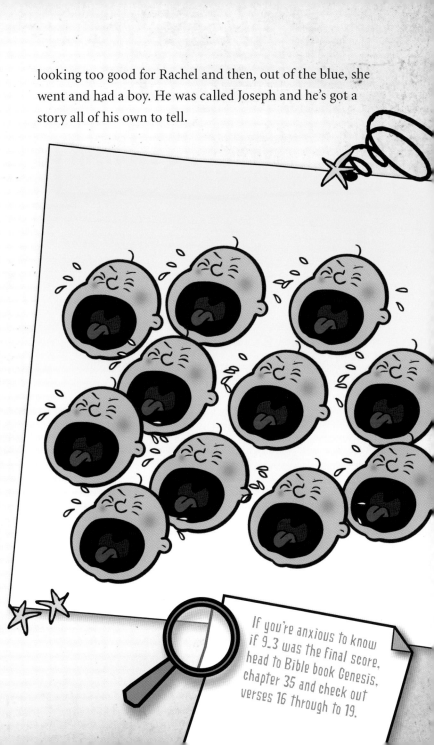

If you're anxious to know if 9-3 was the final score, head to Bible book Genesis, chapter 35 and check out verses 16 through to 19.

5
POTTY MRS POTIPHAR

Joseph (famous for his coloured coat) had been sold into slavery in far away Egypt. His boss, Potiphar (one of the King of Egypt's officers) quickly took a shine to hardworking Joe, and in no time at all he rose through the ranks in Potiphar's household. The Bible says his meteoric rise was down to one thing. God was with Joseph. That was the secret of his success. Joseph was a young man who put God first and did his best to live a life that pleased Him.

Joseph was soon put in charge of the whole show and ended up overseeing the running of the house. Everything was going well for Joseph until Potiphar's wife started eyeing up her handsome slave boy.

Joseph smelt danger and did all in his power to avoid the advances of his master's wife. No way was he going to let down Potiphar or, for that matter, God. One day, when all the men of the house were out and about, Potiphar's wife seized the opportunity and tried to lure Joe into her bedroom. Joseph was having none of it and scarpered as fast as his legs could carry him. But not before his mistress had managed to grab his cloak and use it as evidence to convince her hubbie that Joseph had attempted to seduce his wife (even though he hadn't).

To find out what became of poor, stitched up Joseph, make your way to Bible book Genesis, chapter 39 and verses 19 to 23.

GO, GO, MO!

Moses had an unusual childhood. He'd been born as an Israelite slave (in Egypt) but brought up in the household of Egypt's Pharaoh. I haven't got time to fill you in on how it all happened, so you'll just have to take my word for it.

It must have been difficult for Moses growing up in the royal palace while his fellow Israelites suffered as slaves. The Bible tells us that when Moses had grown up he came across an Israelite slave being beaten by an Egyptian. Perhaps Moses had remembered God's promise that His people wouldn't always be slaves and that one day they'd be freed. Who knows what was going through his mind at that moment. Maybe he thought that he was God's man to set the Israelites free. Moses stepped in to rescue the Israelite slave and in the process ending up killing the Egyptian. Oops! Moses buried the dead man in the sand and made a quick exit.

Word soon got out about what had happened. Next day, when Moses attempted to break up a fight between a couple of Israelite men, one of them turned it back on him and asked Moses what right he had to be lording it over them. 'Do you mean to kill me as you killed the Egyptian?' one of them asked. Yikes! His game was up. If the Israelites knew that he'd killed an Egyptian, it wouldn't be long before Pharaoh found out. Moses took to his heels, hot-footed it and headed for the land of Midian.

To see how this wild story ends, check out Bible book Exodus, chapter 2 and verses 15 through to 22.

CRAZY COUNTDOWN

I t's not every day that God shows up with a couple of angels and they sit down to dinner with you. Well, that's exactly what happened to Abraham and his wife Sarah.

While Sarah was left to do the washing up, Abraham's visitors made tracks for the nearby cities of Sodom and Gomorrah. Sodom was where Abraham's nephew Lot lived, and although Lot was a guy who lived a life that pleased God, hardly anyone else there did. The cities had become a byword for wickedness. God was going to check out if things were really as bad as they were made out to be and, if so, He was planning to destroy the cities. Abraham had a question for God. Tentatively he asked that, just supposing there were fifty people who lived to please God in Sodom and Gomorrah, would God spare the cities from being obliterated? Being the fair-minded God that He is, God said that of course He would.

Abraham had another question to ask God. How about if there were forty-five people who pleased God? Would that sway it? God gave the same answer. Yes, if there were that number of good people living there He'd hold back from wiping them out.

Abraham was on good terms with God but even he didn't take talking to God lightly. His approach might have seemed a little bit forward, but Abraham was also a very humble fella, so he kept pressing God it bit more. What if there were thirty or maybe even twenty? If there were that few righteous inhabitants in the cities, would God cancel His demolition plans? Yep, He sure would.

To find out how few God-pleasing people Abraham managed to persuade God to save the cities for, you'll need to do your own detective work. Look up Bible book Genesis, chapter 18 and verses 32 and 33.

8
BALDY BAITING BACKFIRES

ere's a wild and whacky Bible story that should be a lesson to every kid out there. Elisha was one of God's top prophets and wherever he went, miracles and unusual stuff happened. Elisha had just taken over from a chap called Elijah, who'd been whisked up to heaven without even dying. Strange but true!

Straight after this, Elisha had rocked up in the city of Jericho to be met with the news that the city's water supply was polluted and that women were losing babies in child birth as a result. Elisha ordered that some salt be put into a new bowl and for it to be brought to him. Elisha went to the city's spring and chucked the salt into the water. On God's behalf he commanded that the water become pure and, sure enough, it did. This wasn't simply a temporary fix. The Bible says that the water stayed unpolluted.

As if that wasn't wild enough, check out what happened next. Elisha headed up out of Jericho in the direction of a place called Bethel. Along the way a gang of kids began to taunt our main man and have a laugh at his expense. 'Get out of here, Baldy!' they shouted. Oh, dear. Bad move kids. You don't mess with a guy like Elisha and expect to get away with it.

Elisha spun around and gave them the evils. Having cursed the lot of 'em, find out the wild end to this story by checking it out for yourself. Go to Bible book 2 Kings, chapter 2 and verse 24. Be warned!

TRICK STICK

Moses had been hand-picked by God to tell Egypt's Pharaoh to let His Israelite slaves go free. But first he was gonna need to convince the Israelite leaders that God had sent him.

God pointed to the wooden stick that Moses was holding and told him to throw it down on the ground. Instantly, it turned into a slithering snake. Whoah! Moses carefully grabbed it by the tail and it turned back into a wooden stick. That should convince the Israelite leaders that Moses was God's main man, but just in case they were a bit slow on the uptake, God had another trick up His sleeve. He instructed Moses to slip his hand inside his robe, which he did. When Moses pulled his hand out, it was diseased and covered in white spots. Ugh! Moses put his yukky hand back inside his robe and when he pulled it out again (a roll of the drums, please) … Da-dah … it was healthy! Wow! If Israel's top bods still weren't convinced that God had sent Moses, God told him to pour some water from the River Nile on the ground and it would turn to blood.

You'd think that having seen some of the wild stuff God had done, Moses would be full of confidence, but nope.

He pointed out to God that he wasn't exactly the world's most gifted speaker. God was beginning to get a wee bit ticked off by Moses' whinging, but He wasn't about to have His plan to free the Israelites scuppered by Moses' lack of public-speaking skills.

God suggested that Moses' brother Aaron do the talking. He had the gift of the gab. Moses could tell him what to say and Aaron could blab it. Job done. Off the pair headed to Egypt to set the Israelites free.

Were the Israelite leaders convinced by the miracles Moses performed? Scoot off to Bible book Exodus, chapter 4 and verses 29 to 31.

10
SCAREDY SCOUTS

If you think spies are a modern invention then think again. The Israelites were getting all geared up to enter the land of Canaan, which God had given them to conquer and settle in. Twelve spies were dispatched to check out what the place was like and what sort of opposition they were likely to face.

For forty days the daring dozen darted about eyeing up Canaan. When they finally returned, the spies reported to Moses (the leader of the Israelites) what they'd seen. On the plus side, the land was brilliant for growing things, and to prove it they'd brought back a humungous bunch of grapes which needed two of them to carry it. The downside was that the inhabitants of Canaan were powerful people who lived in fortified cities. It didn't stop there. Just to make matters worse, there were giants living in the land. Gulp! That soon put the wind up the Israelites. No way were they going to invade Canaan if that's what they were up against.

Caleb (one of the twelve spies) wasn't having any of the other Israelites's lily-livered nonsense. He figured that if God had given them the land, a few giants or some fortified cities weren't gonna stop 'em. But, with the exception of Caleb and another spy called Joshua, the rest of the spies

were planning to go nowhere.

Fear and panic quickly spread like wildfire through the Israelite camp. God was well cheesed off with the Israelites for not putting their trust in Him. If they didn't want to take possession of the land that He was giving them then all the moaners and complainers would die in the desert where they were living.

As for the ten spies who'd spread fear and doubt in the Israelite camp, well let's see what God had in store for them. You'll find the verdict in Numbers, chapter 14 and verses 36 to 38.

11
JOSH DUPED

Joshua and the Israelite army were advancing slowly but surely through the land of Canaan, conquering it one city at a time. Word was out that the Israelites meant business, and to make things worse, God was on their side. They were unstoppable.

The people of Gibeon were scared witless and hit upon a crafty plan to avoid being wiped out by Joshua's mighty militia. The Gibeonites loaded up some donkeys with worn-out sacks, patched-up wine skins and mouldy old bread, and sent a posse of them in raggedy clothes to have a head-to-head with the Israelites. The idea was to use these things to trick Joshua into believing that they were from a far-away place. If they were near neighbours from Canaan then they'd be for it, but if they were from a distant land, Joshua wouldn't have any interest in fighting against them.

Guess what? Joshua fell for their trickery, hook, line and sinker. He made a treaty of friendship with the Gibeonites and promised not to kill them. Three days later the Israelites found out that they'd been well and truly duped. Because Joshua and Co. had made a solemn promise before God not to harm the Gibeonites, their hands were tied.

Joshua wasn't going to let the guileful Gibeonites get the upper hand. Look up Bible book Joshua, chapter 9 and verses 22 and 23 to see what he did next.

RA-RA-RUTH!

Naomi, her hubbie Elimelech and their two boys had left Bethlehem (in the land of Judah) because of a famine, and ended up in Moab. Sadly, Elimelech died leaving Naomi and her kids all on their lonesome in a foreign land. All say 'Aaah'. The good news is that her boys (Mahlon and Chilion) ended up marrying a couple of local gals (Orpah and Ruth), but ten years down the line the poor chaps died as well.

Back in Judah things were looking good, and so Naomi decided that now was a good time to head back home to Bethlehem. She bid her fond farewells to her daughters-in-law and tried to persuade them that it was best if they didn't go with her. Orpah and Naomi parted company but Ruth had other ideas. Wherever her mother-in-law went, she'd go. Naomi's people would be her people. Naomi's God would be her God. Naomi realised that Ruth had the bit between her teeth and wasn't going to take no for an answer, so off the pair headed for Bethlehem.

They arrived in Bethlehem just as the barley fields were being harvested. Ruth offered to collect up some of the corn that had been left by the harvest workers. Of all the wild co-incidences, the field belonged to a rich relative of Naomi's

called Boaz. The long and the short of it is that Naomi's loyal daughter-in-law ended up getting married to wealthy Boaz (nice one, Ruth!), but that's not the wildest part of this Bible story.

Ruth might have begun life as a lowly Moabite, but look whose great grandmother she ended up becoming. Check out Bible book Matthew, chapter 1 and verses 5 and 6 to find out.

13
HELLO!
IS ANYONE THERE?

Samuel's mum Hannah had been desperate for a child. She promised God that if she had a son, his life would be dedicated to Him. One time, when she was praying to God in Jerusalem's Temple, Eli the priest gave her the news that she'd been waiting for. God had heard her prayers and she was going to have a son.

When the baby was born they named the lad Samuel, and Hannah told her hubbie Elkanah about her promise to God. He had no choice but to allow his wife to have her way. While he was still very young, Hannah took Samuel to the Temple and handed him over to the care of Eli the priest. Each year Hannah and Elkanah would visit Samuel and take with them a little robe for him to wear as he served God in the Temple. God was kind to Hannah and gave her three more sons and two daughters to make up for allowing Samuel to serve Him.

All the while, Eli's sons (who also worked in the Temple) were up to no good. God had a message for Eli about his wayward sons and he chose young Sam to deliver it. Samuel was sleeping in the heart of the Temple when he was awoken by somebody calling to him. The lad raced off to Eli check out what he wanted. Eli was bemused. He hadn't said anything. So Samuel went back to bed. Once again, he heard a voice calling his name. If you hadn't guessed already, it was God, but Samuel had never heard God speaking to him before so he hadn't a clue what God sounded like. He headed off to Eli again but, just like before, Eli denied having anything to do with it. For the third time Samuel went back to bed and, surprise, surprise, he was woken up once more by someone calling to him. At last the penny dropped and Samuel twigged that it was none other than God speaking.

If you want to know what the message God wanted Samuel to deliver to Eli was, here's where you'll find it. Bible book 1 Samuel, chapter 3 and verses 11 through 14.

14
SAUL THE FOOL

The Israelites (God's special nation) had just got themselves a king, even though God had warned them that it would be much better if they didn't. King Saul was first to rule Israel, and it didn't take long for things to go pear-shaped.

The Israelites were off to fight their arch enemies, the Philistines. King Saul's son (Jonathan) wasted no time in killing the commander of the Philistine army, which really riled Israel's enemy. Grrrrr! They were seething mad. Thirty thousand chariots, six thousand horsemen and more Philistine soldiers than you could ever count, lined up to attack the Israelites. It was a walkover. The Israelites were completely out-numbered and out-manoeuvred. They fled for their lives and hid wherever they could; in caves, holes, pits, wells or behind rocks. The lucky ones managed to escape across the River Jordan, but Saul and loads of his men were trapped and desperate.

Samuel (a prophet of God) had sent word that he'd be showing up within the week. The king waited and waited. His troops were deserting him by the droves. What was he to do? When the seven days were up and there was still no

sign of Samuel, Saul took things into his own hands and sacrificed some animals to God in the hope of turning things around. Big mistake! Doing the sacrifices was Samuel's job. Even Israel's king wasn't allowed to do it. As promised, Samuel did in fact turn up that day, and when he did, he gave King Saul such an ear-bashing and told him what a foolish thing he'd done.

Scurry to Bible book 1 Samuel, chapter 13 and verses 13 to 14 to hear what else Samuel had to say.

15
DAVE'S CAVE

King Saul (of Israel) was on the prowl. He was hunting high and low for a fella called David, who God had lined up as his replacement. Saul's days as king were numbered because he'd made such a hash of things, and now the thought of popular David filling his royal shoes was more than he could bear. King Saul was insanely jealous of David and wanted him dead.

We catch up with them as Saul and three thousand of his tiptop fighting men were scouring the countryside for David. For his part, David and his men were hiding deep inside a cave, hoping to evade capture. King Saul, meanwhile, was desperate for the loo, so he popped in to spend a penny in the very same cave where David was holed up. David's men couldn't believe their luck. Here was their chance to kill Saul before he got them. David tip-toed up behind the king and snipped off the corner of his robe without Saul knowing.

Immediately David felt overwhelmed by guilt. What had he done? Saul might have fouled up but he was still king of Israel in God's eyes, and even to think of harming him was wrong. As King Saul left the cave David raced after him and confessed what he'd done.

Did Saul seize David and kill him? Go to Bible book 1 Samuel, chapter 24 and verses 16 through to 22 to find out.

16 KING'S CONUNDRUM

I f you could ask God for absolutely anything you wanted, what would it be? Hmm! Well, while you're having a good old ponder, let me tell you about King Solomon and what he asked for from God.

Solomon had taken over from his dad David as Israel's king, and what a difficult job it was. The Israelites were God's special nation, whose job it was to demonstrate to other people what God was like. They didn't always find it the easiest thing and often as not wanted to do their own thing rather than what God wanted. The king's job was to rule the nation in a way that pleased God, so he generally had his work cut out.

One night, shortly after Solomon had offered sacrifices to God, he had a dream in which God appeared to him. God asked King Solomon the same question I asked you. 'What would you like Me to give you?' Wow! What an offer. Did God really mean *anything*? He sure did. I suppose he could plump for the latest model of chariot, or how about a spanking new home, or maybe oodles and oodles of gold and silver? Solomon had a bit of a think about it and then came up with an answer that made God's day.

Solomon was still quite young and he was well aware of the responsibilities of ruling Israel, so he asked God to give him the wisdom to rule God's nation fairly and also the ability to know good from bad. In fact, God was so chuffed with Solomon's answer that He decided to give the king some other goodies as well. Want to find out what they were?

Of course you do. Head off to Bible book 1 Kings, chapter 3 and verses 10 to 14 to find out.

17
JAMMY JAR

The Bible is full of jaw-dropping miracles and this story is one of them. Elisha worked for God as one of His prophets. Prophets are people who hear what God is saying and then pass on the info to others. Prophets were usually power-packed (with God's power) so they could back up what they had to say with a miracle or two to convince people that it was really God speaking. Elisha was about to have one of those times.

A widow had rocked up at Elisha's place with a sad sob story. Her hubbie had gone and died, leaving her with a heap of debt. She didn't have a bean, so the person the money was owed to was threatening to take away her two sons to be his slaves as payment. The poor widow was distraught. Elisha asked if she had anything at all that she could give the man. Except for a small jar of olive oil she had nothing. Absolutely zilch!

Elisha had a plan. He told the widow to borrow as many empty jars from her neighbours as she could lay her hands on. Next up, he instructed her to shut herself indoors and start pouring the olive oil from her small jar into the empty jars. With the help of her two boys she kept pouring and pouring until each and every jar was brimful. As they filled the very last jar, the oil stopped flowing. Wild or what!

Was there enough oil to pay off her debt? Your answer is to be found in Bible book 2 Kings, chapter 4 and verse 7.

SUPER SAMSON

Who's your favourite superhero? Superman? Spiderman? Batman? Well, for your info, the Bible also features superheroes, and Samson was one of them.

Samson was one of Israel's leaders and God had given him supernatural strength so that he could defeat God's enemies. Between you and me, Samson was a bit of a hothead, but that's probably why God chose him in the first place. Israel was forever at war with the nearby Philistines and then, to put a spanner in the works, Samson went and fell head over heels in love with a Philistine gal. His mum and dad tried to persuade him that marrying one of their enemies wasn't the world's best idea, but Samson wasn't gonna take no for an answer. So the three of them headed off to Timnah (where the girl lived) to sort things out for the wedding.

Along the way Samson heard the roar of a young lion and went off in search of it. Suddenly God's power came on him and he tore the lion to pieces with his bare hands. Awesome! Job done, Samson went back to his mum and dad as if nothing had happened. The wedding plans were made and a few days later Samson returned to claim his bride.

A surprising sight met his eyes and you can discover what it was for yourself. Look up Bible book Judges, chapter 14 and verses 8 to 9.

19
JOASH MAKES A HASH

Joash was king of Judah, and the Bible says that he was a good king. A lot of the credit for that goes to a guy called Jehoiada, who was a priest in God's Temple in Judah. Jehoiada helped to keep the king on the straight and narrow with God.

One of Joash's good decisions was to make repairs to the Temple, which was looking a little the worse for wear. To fund this enterprise Joash decided to dip into the money that the priests collected from people who made sacrifices at the Temple. It was a good idea, but for whatever reason none of the money ever made its way to repairing the place. Joash was having none of it. He called an emergency meeting of the priests and asked them what was going on. King Joash soon realised that leaving the priests to collect money for the repairs was not going to work, so he hit upon the idea of putting a big money box right next to the altar in the Temple. When the worshippers handed over their cash the priests had to put it in the money box, then and there. Once the box was full the royal secretary counted it up and then handed it over to the builders and craftsmen so they could get on with the job of doing the repairs. This idea worked much better and over time the Temple was restored to its former glory.

When Jehoiada died, Joash lost the plot in a big way. He started to allow his people to worship any old god they pleased. God sent prophets to warn the king that he was on dodgy ground, but Joash simply ignored them. He even had one of them (Zechariah) stoned to death. God had had enough of this nonsense and was calling time on Joash's reign as king.

Read about how the king met his end in Bible book 2 Chronicles, chapter 24 and verses 23 through to 25.

SOLOMON THE CELEB

E veryone seems to want to be famous these days, but King Solomon (from the Bible) was a big celebrity without the help of TV appearances. God had given Solomon bucket-loads of wisdom, which meant he could rule his nation (Israel) really well. The upshot of this was that Israel hit the big time and was successful in everything it turned its hand to. Nothing was in short supply and the king was rolling in it.

Solomon was so wise and so rich that news of him spread far and wide. One lady (the queen of Sheba) packed her bags and trekked mega miles to meet Solomon face to face and to check out if everything she'd heard about him was true. The queen didn't come empty-handed. She showed up with camel-loads of spices, jewels and gold to give to Israel's king. The queen of Sheba sure wasn't disappointed by what she heard and saw. The opulence and wealth took her breath away. She quizzed Solomon about anything and everything, and each time he came up with an answer. Such was his amazing wisdom that nothing she asked had him stumped. The queen was blown away by her visit to Solomon but if her camels thought they'd be travelling back to Sheba with a lighter load, they were going to need to think again.

Go to Bible book 1 Kings, chapter 10 and verse 13 to see what I'm on about.

ALL'S WELL THAT ENDS WELL

Jeremiah (a prophet of God) had been banging on about the way the people of Judah (where he lived) had turned their backs on God. Time and time again he warned them that if they didn't turn from their wicked ways, God would punish them by allowing their land to be captured by the Babylonians.

Hardly anybody took a blind bit of notice of what Jeremiah had to say, even when the Babylonian army surrounded Judah's capital city (Jerusalem). As the inhabitants of the city held on for dear life, hoping that the Babylonians would go away, Jeremiah was flung into prison to shut him up. When he was eventually released, Jeremiah started spreading his warnings of doom and destruction all over again. The king's officials complained that Jeremiah was a loose cannon and he wasn't doing anything for the morale of the hard-pressed people of Jerusalem. They persuaded the king (Zedekiah) that it would be best for all concerned if Jeremiah was killed, and pronto. Using ropes, the scheming officials lowered Jeremiah to the foot of a dry well (except for the sludgy mud at the bottom) and left him there to die.

Not everyone was against Jeremiah. Ebedmelech (who worked in the royal palace) had a word with Zedekiah and managed to convince him that leaving one of God's prophets to die of starvation in a well was a bad move. With the help of three men, Ebedmelech was given permission to hoist a rather muddy Jeremiah back up out of the well.

Did the people of Judah finally listen to Jeremiah's warnings? Check out Bible book Jeremiah, chapter 39 and read verses 1 through to 10 to see for yourself.

FOR THE CHOP

King Nebuchadnezzar ruled Babylon with a rod of iron, and woe betided anyone who crossed him. As far as Nebuchadnezzar was concerned, he was a god and should be worshipped. God took a different view and had shown the king (in a dream) what he thought of his big ego. The dream featured a massive tree that grew and grew until it reached the sky so that you couldn't miss it, wherever you lived. The tree was loaded down with enough fruit to feed everyone. Suddenly, an angel announced that the tree was going to be chopped down and that just a stump would be left.

The dream really put the wind up Nebuchadnezzar and he was desperate to find out what it meant. None of his magicians or astrologers had a clue what the dream was about, so the king called for Daniel (also known as Belteshazzar). Daniel worshipped God and He'd given him the ability to interpret dreams. When Daniel heard the dream he was somewhat alarmed. He explained to Nebuchadnezzar that the tree in fact represented the king himself. He had grown so great that his power extended over the whole earth. But God was calling time on his tyrannical rule and he was going to be driven out of the city to live like an animal for seven years. Daniel did give the king a get-out clause. If he turned from his wicked ways God would make sure that none of this stuff happened.

Make your way to Bible book Daniel, chapter 4 and verses 29 to 33 to find out how the king responded.

23

VERY TEMPTING

How would you fancy going without food for forty days? Not much, I reckon. Well, that's precisely what Jesus did right after He'd been baptised in the River Jordan.

Filled with God's power, Jesus was getting ready to reveal Himself as God's Son. His mission was to patch things up between people and God, but first Jesus needed to be tested to make sure He was fit for the job. Jesus could only do what God required if He was perfect, which meant He couldn't so much as do one teensy thing wrong. That might sound completely impossible to you and me, but don't forget that Jesus is God. Who was going to put Jesus to the test? None other than God's number one enemy, Satan. If Jesus succeeded in His mission to planet Earth, Satan would be defeated. The battle was on.

After forty foodless days in the hot and sticky desert, Satan showed up. 'If you're God's Son, order these stones to turn to bread.' Satan was quoting bits of the Bible at Jesus but Jesus wasn't gonna give in to God's words being twisted. Jesus immediately came back at Satan with a Bible bit of His own: 'The Bible says that man cannot live on bread alone but by every word that God speaks.' Good move, Jesus! 1–0 to Jesus.

Satan had another go at trying to tempt Jesus away from doing what God wanted. He tried to persuade Jesus to leap off the highest part of God's Temple (in Jerusalem) and trust in God's angels to protect Him. Once again, Jesus held His ground and fired back another Bible bit to counterattack Satan's temptation. 2–0 to Jesus.

Satan had one more trick up his sleeve. He offered Jesus all the kingdoms of the world on one condition ... that He worship Satan.

Did Jesus give in to Satan's tempting temptations? Check out Bible book Matthew, chapter 4 and verses 10 and 11 to discover all.

THE BATTLE OF THE BUILDERS

If you know anything about the Jewish people, you'll be well aware that Jerusalem (their capital city) was very special to them. Sad to say, Jerusalem had been destroyed by invaders and the inhabitants captured and taken to a foreign land. One of the exiles (Nehemiah) had done well for himself and had ended up as a servant in the royal palace. News reached Nehemiah that his beloved Jerusalem's walls were falling down, so he summoned up all the courage he could muster and asked the king (Artaxerxes) if he'd let him go back to repair them. Amazingly, the king said 'Yes' to Nehemiah's wild idea, and sent him on his way with an armed escort and made sure he had all the building materials to complete the task.

On his arrival in Jerusalem, Nehemiah soon realised that he had a big job on his hands. Jerusalem lay in ruins. Its gates had been burned and the walls were crumbling. With God's help Nehemiah set about turning things round. He rallied the support of every Jewish person he could find. Each family was given a job to do and nobody got away with doing nothing. From the richest to the poorest, everyone was expected to roll up their sleeves and muck in.

Just when things were getting under way, Sanballat, Tobiah and Geshem (enemies of the Jews) decided that they didn't like the idea of Jerusalem being rebuilt, and tried every dirty trick in the book to stop it. They spread rumours that the Jewish people were planning a revolt, they ridiculed Nehemiah's rebuilding plan and said it wouldn't work, and they even attempted to lure Nehemiah away to kill him – but the work went on. Nehemiah and his fellow Jews remained armed and alert. No way was anyone gonna stop them.

Did Nehemiah have his dream of restoring Jerusalem fulfilled or was it scuppered by Sanballat and his cunning conspirators? Find out in Bible book Nehemiah, chapter 6 and verse 15 and 16.

25
ESTHER TO THE RESCUE

King Xerxes ruled over his vast empire from the city of Susa. Along the way he'd conquered and captured the Jewish nation. The king and his wife Queen Vashti had fallen out with each other and Xerxes thought it was about time he got himself another queen. He dispatched his servants to scour the land for a beautiful new bride to replace Vashti. All the young hopefuls were brought back to the palace and prepared for a meet up with the king.

The girl Xerxes eventually picked to be his new queen was called Esther. Esther was a Jew but she didn't let on to the king. One day, her uncle Mordecai overheard a plot to kill Xerxes, reported it and the would-be assassins were executed. Soon after this, a guy called Haman got promoted by King Xerxes, but much to Haman's annoyance Mordecai refused to bow down to him. Haman was well mad and hatched a plan to kill not only Mordecai (on a gallows) but all the Jews in the land.

Mordecai secretly visited Esther to warn her of what Haman was up to. It was time for Esther to blow her cover. Esther persuaded the king to have Haman invited to a

special banquet. When the day arrived, Haman thought
he'd hit the big time. A banquet specially for him. Wow!
Little did he know that the queen was about to set him up.
During the meal she asked Haman what should be done
for a man the king wanted to honour. Thinking that she
was referring to him, Haman suggested a regal procession
on horseback through Susa. Esther then told the king
about Mordecai saving his life and so it was he who got the
victory lap of the city and Haman was the one who ended
up leading him round.

When it was all over Haman felt humiliated, but worse
was still to come. Esther invited Haman back to the palace
again and this time she snitched on him to the king, telling
Xerxes all about the
wicked plot to kill
the Jewish people
… of which she
was one!

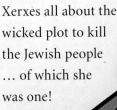

The king was furious with Haman
and if you want to find out the
wild twist to this story, here's
what you do. Head for Bible book
Esther, chapter 7 and verse 10.

26
FANTASTIC FAITH

Jesus never needed much persuading to heal sick people because that was one of the jobs God had sent Him to do. The land Jesus lived in (Israel) was under Roman rule at the time, which meant that it was swarming with Roman soldiers. One time, when Jesus rolled up in a place called Capernaum, a Roman soldier (a centurion) made a beeline for Him and asked Jesus to heal his sick servant. The sick servant was paralysed but the centurion was in no doubt that Jesus was the Man to get him back on his feet again.

Jesus was about to set off to heal the man when the centurion stopped Him in His tracks. The centurion told Jesus that he wasn't worthy to have someone as awesome as Him in his house. He knew that Jesus had been sent by God so He had God's authority and power to do anything He wanted. How about if Jesus just gave the command for his servant to get better. That should do the trick; after all, as a soldier he knew full well what it was like to be both under authority and also to have people do what he commanded. Couldn't Jesus just do the same? Jesus was flabbergasted at the centurion's wild suggestion but He went ahead and healed his servant there and then.

Jesus had something else to say about this Roman soldier. Check out what it was in Bible book Matthew, chapter 8 and verse 10.

27

LOUD CROWD NOT ALLOWED

The clock was ticking and Jesus knew that He didn't have much time left on planet Earth. Jesus was on a mission from God and the stage was being set for His big finale in Israel's capital city Jerusalem. Everywhere Jesus went crowds flocked to hear what He had to say and to see the miracles He did. When He showed up in Jerusalem for one last time it was the same story.

As Jesus got closer to the city He dispatched a couple of His trusty disciples to a nearby village to fetch a colt. When the pair arrived it was just as Jesus had told them. As they were untying the colt outside a doorway, some of the villagers asked what they were doing. When the disciples mentioned Jesus' name they let the pair carry on. How did Jesus know they'd find the animal there? The Bible doesn't answer that question but it does say that this very day had been predicted by one of God's prophets way back in the mists of time.

The disciples covered the colt with their cloaks and helped Jesus on to it. It didn't take much time for a large crowd to

gather. People began to cover the road ahead with their cloaks and the leaves of palm trees. The crowd were treating Jesus as if He were some kind of king, but whoever heard of a king arriving at a city riding on a colt? In a horse-drawn carriage, maybe, but not the colt of a lowly donkey.

Jesus knew exactly what He was doing. Sure, He was a king, but a king of the like they'd never seen before (and never would again!). As Jesus rode into Jerusalem, people shouted out their praise to Him. 'Hosanna in the highest!' 'Blessed is He who comes in the name of the Lord!' Meanwhile, the religious leaders (who by and large didn't like Jesus) were getting a bit hot under the collar. They wanted His disciples and the crowd to quit cheering Jesus.

Want to know Jesus' sharp reply to them? Go to Bible book Luke, chapter 19 and verse 40 to see what it was.

28

FINAL FEAST

The Jewish people have loads of different feasts and festivals to help remind them of stuff that God has done. The Passover Feast was one of them. It was all about remembering how God had rescued the Israelites from being slaves in Egypt.

We catch up with Jesus and His twelve disciples (His band of followers) as they celebrate the Passover in an upstairs room in the city of Jerusalem. As they reclined around the table, Jesus dropped the bombshell that one of them was going to betray Him. What? He must be mistaken. Nope. Jesus said that whoever dipped his hand into one of the bowls of food at the same time as He did was the culprit. Jesus also warned that whoever did the dirty deed to double-cross Him, was making a mega mistake and it was such a bad thing that it would be better for him if he'd never even been born.

To cut a long story short, it was Judas (their treasurer), and as soon as they'd finished eating he legged it. Jesus knew full well that Judas was going to hand Him over to the religious leaders, who wanted His guts for garters, but He carried on with the meal regardless. Jesus used the Passover wine and bread to tell His close buddies that He was going to allow His body to be killed and His blood to spill out as a sacrifice to God to get rid of all the grot in the world. For your info, it was the very last meal Jesus had with these guys before He died.

Take a look at Bible book Mark, chapter 14 and verse 26 to discover one last thing Jesus and the disciples all did together.

29

DOZING DISCIPLES

This wild Bible story happens the night before Jesus was executed. Jesus (with His disciples in tow) was headed for a place called Gethsemane, just outside the city of Jerusalem. As soon as they'd arrived, Jesus sat most of His followers down, but took three of them (Peter, James and John) off to pray with Him. Jesus was having a hard time, knowing what He was going to have to face the next day, and He needed the support of His close friends.

Having filled them in with how bad He was feeling, Jesus left the three disciples and fell face down on the ground to pray. There was nothing Jesus wanted more than to do what His Father in heaven (God) asked of Him, but it still didn't make the thought of facing death any easier. On His return, Jesus found Peter and the others sound asleep. Couldn't they even stay awake with Him for an hour?

For a second time Jesus went off to wrestle in prayer, and when He came back that time, guess what? His disciples were snoozing again. To be fair, it had been a long day and they were exhausted.

Check out if Jesus' followers were able to stir themselves to support their Master. Go to Bible book Matthew, chapter 26 and verse 44 to 46 to enlighten yourself.

BODY BOTHER

30

The story so far is that Jesus had died after being executed by the Romans (but goaded on by Israel's religious leaders). However, loads of people thought that He was the best thing since sliced bread (not that sliced bread had actually been invented then). One of them was a rich chap called Joseph (from Arimathea). As night was drawing in, Joseph showed up at the Roman governor's place and asked Pilate (the Roman governor) if he could have Jesus' body so he could give it a proper burial. Joseph took Jesus' body away to be buried. Not being short of a penny or two meant that Joseph already owned a tomb for when he died. Once he'd laid Jesus inside, Joseph sealed the tomb with a whopping big stone.

Next day, the religious leaders suddenly had a thought. Hadn't Jesus said stuff about coming back to life in three days? They figured that all it would take was Jesus' disciples to nick the body and everyone would think the predictions had come true. They weren't going to stand for any of that nonsense. Jesus had given them a hard time while He was alive. The last thing they needed was Jesus being a thorn in their side from beyond the grave. The religious leaders scurried off to Pilate to fill him in on their fears.

Want to find out the wild lengths the religious leaders went to to make sure Jesus' body stayed in the tomb? Look up Bible book Matthew, chapter 27 and read verses 65 and 66.

31

BELLOWING BART

Jesus spent most of His time criss-crossing Israel, telling the Jewish people about God and doing miracles and stuff to demonstrate that God cared about 'em. One particular time, Jesus was on His way out of Jericho, accompanied by His loyal disciples and an adoring crowd of hangers-on. It must have been chaos.

Sitting by the roadside was a poor blind beggar called Bartimaeus (which, if you're interested, means 'son of Timaeus'). When word reached Bartimaeus that Jesus was in town, he hollered at the top of his voice to grab Jesus' attention. He must have been making a right old din because the Bible says that people tried to shut him up. Did Bartimaeus take any notice? He most certainly didn't. In fact, he yelled all the louder until he had Jesus' attention.

Jesus stopped in His tracks and sent some folk to fetch the blind beggar. Bartimaeus jumped to his feet and was led to Jesus. 'What do you want Me to do for you?' Jesus asked him. A pretty obvious question, you might think, but Jesus wanted to know that Bartimaeus really trusted Him. No surprises for guessing that Bartimaeus wanted his sight back.

OK, so let me tell you that he did get what he wanted, but to find out what it was that made his healing a dead cert, you're gonna need to head to your Bibles. Check out Bible book Mark, chapter 10 and verse 52 to see what Jesus had to say to Bart.

32
FUNNY MONEY

Heaps of the stories in the Bible are set in and around
Jerusalem (Israel's capital city). At the heart of Jerusalem
was the Temple where God was worshipped and where
sacrifices were made to Him. The people of Israel (the Jews)
were expected to contribute to the upkeep of the Temple and
to pay for the priests who served there, day in, day out. Jesus
often hung out at the Temple, and we catch up with Him (and
His disciples) as they do just that.

Jesus had plonked Himself down, slap-bang opposite
the place (called the Temple treasury) where visitors to
the Temple put their offerings. The Temple was heaving,
and a steady stream of Jews passed by the treasury to
drop their gifts in for all to see. The more someone had to
give, the bigger the show they could make of it. Although
loads of rich people chucked in mega amounts of dosh,
not everyone's bank account was a bottomless pit. A poor
widow sidled up to the money box and dropped in just two
teensy copper coins, which were worth next to nothing.
Jesus didn't miss a trick and had seen what she'd given
towards the running costs of God's Temple. He quickly
rallied His disciples to discuss what He'd just witnessed.

Was Jesus mad at the widow for being a miser? Check out for yourself the wild stuff Jesus had to say about the lady. Go to Bible book Mark, chapter 12 and verses 43 and 44.

33
DINNER TIME DILEMMAS

Having Jesus round for dinner was always a risky business. You never knew quite what He'd do or say. Jesus had taken up an invitation to dine at the home of a top religious bod, and all eyes were on Jesus to see what He'd do.

It didn't take long for Jesus to spring into action. Right in front of Him was a sick man He planned to heal. Just one small problem. It was the Jewish Sabbath day, which meant that you could barely lift a finger without breaking one of the religious leaders' strict laws, but Jesus didn't have time for many of their petty 'dos' and 'do nots'. Loads of them were just man-made rules and absolutely nothing to do with God at all. Jesus hated stuff that made people's lives a misery, so He asked His host and all the other guests whether healing somebody on the Sabbath was OK to do. Nobody said a dicky bird, so Jesus went ahead and healed the sick man.

Next up, Jesus had a thing or two to say about how all the guests were trying to get the best seats at the table. It was obvious to Jesus that they all had over-inflated egos and

it was about time somebody (namely Him) popped them.
Jesus told them that God saw things differently. People who
thought they were better than others were in for a bit of a
surprise. God would bring them down with a bump, but if
you acted a bit more humbly then He'd do the opposite.

Jesus rounded off His meal-time
lecture with a bit of useful advice
for the next time any of them threw
a dinner party. Discover what it was
in Bible book Luke, chapter 14 and
verses 12 through to 14.

34

POWER ARRANGER

Before Jesus returned to heaven, He gave His followers the job of telling the rest of the world that He'd made it possible for everyone to be friends with God again. Philip was one of the guys who set about doing what Jesus had said.

Good old Philip had made his way from Jerusalem to a place called Samaria. Because God's power was with Philip, he was able to heal loads of people and do loads of miracles to prove that God was really serious about wanting them to be His friends again. Not everyone was over the moon about having Philip centre stage. A local magician (Simon the Sorcerer) had been a bit of a celebrity because of his wizardry, but now people were buying into what Philip had to offer and it looked liked Simon's days of fame were up.

To his credit, Simon was so bowled over by God's power working through Philip that he wanted a slice of the action as well. When a couple of Phil's friends (Peter and John) dropped by to lend a hand, things went wild. Cartloads of Samaritans had become followers of Jesus, but none of them had power from God like Philip. That was all about to change. Peter and John placed their hands on the new

believers and they were also filled with God's awesome power. Wow! Simon was well impressed. If Peter and John could do stuff like that, why couldn't he? Of all the stupid things to do, he offered to give the pair a nice little back-hander if they could just give him the same ability to impart God's power.

Want to hear what Peter had to say to Simon's silly suggestion? Check out Bible book Acts, chapter 8 and verse 20 through to 24.

SHIPWRECK SHAMBLES

35

Paul was a man on a mission to tell as many people as possible about Jesus. Along the way he'd made a fair few enemies and had ended up getting arrested. Paul protested his innocence and as a Roman citizen demanded a fair trial, which is why he was on his way to Rome. Paul and his fellow prisoners were sailing with an armed escort across the Mediterranean Sea but the weather had taken a turn for the worse. Winter was fast approaching and the ship was sheltering on the Greek island of Crete, but the harbour was no good for spending the winter. The decision was made to sail round the island to somewhere a bit more suitable. Soon after they'd set sail a hurricane-force gale caught them by surprise and drove the ship out to sea. The storm was so bad the crew had to hold the ship together with ropes just to stop it breaking up into pieces. Things went from bad to worse. The sky was as black as night and the ship's crew feared ever seeing daylight, let alone dry land, ever again. Just when everyone thought that all hope was lost Paul had an unexpected visitor. One of God's angels turned up and told Paul that God would protect him and everyone on the ship. All 276 of 'em would survive but the ship was a gonner. Sure enough, after fourteen terrifying days at sea the sailors discovered that they were not far from the shore and decided to run the ship aground on the beach. Before they reached it the ship crashed onto a sandbank and started to break up in the pounding waves.

Did Paul and his travelling companions make it ashore like the angel had promised? Read the final part of Paul's wild adventure in Bible book Acts, chapter 27 and verses 42 through to 44 for an answer.

WOOLLY WANDERER

Most of us like a good story, and Jesus knew that. Rather than hit people over the head with heavy lectures about God, He used clever stories to help them understand different things about Him. For instance, there was one time when Jesus was talking to a bunch of bad guys, and some religious leaders dropped by to listen in on what God's Son had to say. To be honest, the religious leaders hadn't exactly taken a shine to Jesus, and all this mixing with no-hopers and losers was the last straw. Jesus decided to tell a story (the Bible calls it a parable) that would appeal to the no-hopers but would really get up the noses of the religious lot. Here's how it went.

A man has a hundred sheep but one of them goes and wanders off (like sheep do). What's he to do? Is it really worth all the effort of chasing off over the hillsides hunting for his missing mutton? After all, let's be honest, it was the sheep's own stupid fault for wandering off in the first place and anyway, the man would still have ninety-nine sheep left, wouldn't he? Would anyone really miss one measly sheep?

Well, the man in Jesus' story would. He hunts high and low until he finds his woolly wanderer.

What was the point of the story? Find out in Bible book Luke, chapter 15 and verses 4 to 7.

37
SEETHING SILVERSMITHS

One of the most famous fellas from the New Testament bit of the Bible was Paul, partly cos he wrote huge chunks of it and also because he stars in some of it.

Paul was in the city of Ephesus putting all his efforts into trying to persuade its citizens that Jesus was the Son of God. Wherever Paul went he healed the sick and performed mighty miracles in God's power. Over time hordes of Ephesians became believers in Jesus and quit worshipping their man-made gods. Not everyone saw this as a good thing. A chap called Demetrius (a silversmith), who made silver shrines of the Ephesian goddess Artemis, was beginning to feel the pinch. Business was going from bad to worse as more and more people gave up worshipping Artemis. Something had to be done, and fast. Demetrius called an emergency meeting of anyone and everyone whose livelihood had taken a nose dive since Paul had hit town.

His fellow workers were hopping mad with Paul's meddling, and very soon the whole city was in uproar.

'Great is Artemis of the Ephesians!' they chanted. Paul was nowhere to be found, so the angry mob grabbed his travelling companions (Gaius and Aristarchus) and frog-marched them to the city's meeting place. Paul wanted to address the crowd but he was persuaded against doing so. He'd be ripped apart in seconds.

For two hours the Ephesians kept up their chanting until they were eventually quietened down by the city clerk. He reminded the inhabitants of Ephesus that if they had a complaint against Paul they should take him to court. His tactics worked and the crowd dispersed.

Did Paul hang around to risk stirring another commotion? Head for Bible book Acts, chapter 20 and verse 1 to find out.

38
ABRAHAM TO THE RESCUE

Abraham's nephew Lot had gone to live in Sodom. Sodom was one of a few cities that had lived under the thumb of the king of Elam (Kerdorlaomer) for a dozen difficult years, and now the people had had enough. But wait a minute. Not so fast! The king of Elam wasn't in any mood to tolerate a rebellion. He called together three other kings (who were his allies) and set off to show the rebels who was boss.

In a place called the Valley of Siddim, the four kings (and their armies, of course) drew their battle lines against five rebel kings (and their armies, of course). Kerdorlaomer's lot had the upper hand and Lot's lot fled. Unfortunately for them, things only went from bad to worse. That particular valley was full of tar pits and some of Lot's lot fell in 'em. Others fled to the hills but many (including Lot) were taken away as prisoners.

News of Lot's fate soon reached Abraham, who wasted no time. He rallied his 318 fighting men and set off in hot pursuit of his nabbed nephew. At dead of night Abraham's men split up, surrounded the enemy camp and attacked.

Did Abraham's tactics succeed in rescuing Lot? All is revealed in Bible book Genesis, chapter 14 and verses 15 and 16.

39

WISHY WASHY WAVERER

Before Jesus was executed by the Romans He was put on trial by the Roman governor (a man called Pilate). While Pilate tried to find out who Jesus was and what exactly it was that He was standing trial for, the religious leaders (who hated His guts) shouted out all sorts of false accusations against Him. Did Jesus reply to these accusations? No way. He didn't say a word, much to Pilate's astonishment.

The governor was beginning to feel a bit uneasy about having Jesus on his hands and tried to find a way of letting Him go free. Here's an idea. Every year around this time it was the custom to release a prisoner of the people's choice. Was it to be Barabbas (a murderer) or Jesus? Perplexed Pilate thought he'd got himself out of the pickle he was in, but the religious leaders stirred up the crowd to call for the release of Barabbas.

Things weren't going the way Pilate was hoping. To rub salt into the wound, a message from his wife arrived. She was in a right old tizzy because of a dream she'd had about Jesus. Mrs Pilate (sorry, the Bible doesn't tell us her name) told her hubbie to have nothing to do with Jesus. He was an

innocent man. Just what he didn't need to hear.

All the while the religious leaders were stoking up the crowd to a frenzy. They were baying for blood and wanted Jesus executed. Pilate was running out of ideas and starting to panic. No way was he going to be responsible for the death of an innocent man. As a sign that he wanted nothing more to do with this kangaroo court, he washed his hands in front of everyone. From then on what happened to Jesus was on their heads.

To see how this story ends, head for Matthew, chapter 27 and verses 25 and 26.

40
BIG BOOK BOMBSHELL

If you've ever tried to do the splits, you'll know that it can be rather painful. Well, that's the very thing that happened to the nation of Israel a long time ago. It split in two to become Israel and Judah. By and large Judah kept things the way God wanted them because it had God's Temple and the nation's capital city, Jerusalem. Sometimes Judah's kings let things slip and they forgot about God. Then along would come a good king who'd bring the nation back into line with God again.

Josiah was one such king. Josiah was a guy who loved God and did his best to please Him, unlike his dad, Judah's previous king. His dad was into worshipping all sorts of weird gods and encouraged his people to do the same. Josiah soon put a stop to that and destroyed all the places of worship to these gods. He also had God's Temple restored and in the process a special book was discovered by Hilkiah the priest. It was called the Book of the Law and contained God's rules and regulations for His special nation.

When King Josiah clapped eyes on the book he was

horrified. No way had they been keeping these laws and doing what God wanted. Josiah was so upset he deliberately ripped his robes as a sign of how sorry he was. He sent his officials off in search of any prophets of God they could find to see what God had to say about them not keeping His laws.

Word soon came back that God was gonna let Josiah off the hook because he'd humbled himself before God and was sorry. Phew! What a relief. The downside was that sometime in the future (after Josiah had died) God was going to punish Judah, big time, for its disobedience.

Did Josiah let things slip again because he knew he'd got off lightly? Take a look at Bible book 2 Chronicles, chapter 34 and verse 33 to discover all.

41
TOPSY-TURVY TEACHING

Most of you will have heard of a chap called Moses. He was the man God gave a big bunch of laws to for the Israelites to obey. Just for your info, these laws didn't make the Israelites better people, they just showed them the sort of high standards God expects. God's long-term plan was for Jesus (who features in this Bible bit) to change people's hearts so that living God's way would come naturally. As Jesus travelled to and fro around Israel, He began to tell the Jewish people about this.

For instance, the Law said that murdering people was a big no-no. (Sounds OK to me.) But Jesus said that even being angry with someone (we're talking big-time angry here, not just being a little bit cross) means you're gonna be out of line with God. He also said that it now wasn't OK to get your own back if you'd been wronged. If somebody nicked your clothes (not the ones you're wearing, obviously) then let 'em have your coat as well.

Jesus didn't stop there. He also said that if somebody upsets you then you've gotta forgive them. Why? Simple.

Cos God's prepared to forgive all the stuff that we've done wrong. Jesus said that criticising people was out. Stop fault-finding and instead take the microscope to your own life to check out where you're missing the mark yourself.

Jesus dolloped heaps of this sort of teaching into the laps of His listeners to prepare them for the change of heart that He was going to give those who became His followers.

Jesus summed up this topsy-turvy teaching in a nutshell. To see what it was, take a look in Bible book Matthew, chapter 7 and verse 12.

42

ADVANCED WARNING

It might come as a bit of a surprise to you to know that the Bible is jam-packed with adverts. Wild, I know, but completely true. You're probably scratching your head and thinking, 'I can't remember seeing any adverts last time I read the Bible'. Let me put your mind at rest. We're not talking about adverts for things like underarm deodorants or super soft toilet rolls. The real name for these Bible adverts is 'prophecies' and they were written down by people called prophets. Over three hundred of them advertised that Jesus (God's Son) was on His way to planet Earth years before He actually showed up. Here's a few of them so you can see what I'm on about.

For starters, in Bible book Isaiah, chapter 7 and verse 14 it says, '… The virgin will be with child and will give birth to a son, and will call him Immanuel [which means "God with us"].' If you know the Christmas story you'll know that that's exactly what happened. A young virgin (Mary) gave birth to God's Son (Jesus). Another Bible advert pointed out that Jesus was gonna be born in a place called Bethlehem (which He was). 'But you, Bethlehem … out of you will come … one who will be ruler over Israel.' That's from Bible book Micah, chapter 5 and verse 2. Fast-forwarding to the story of Easter, check out this advert from Bible book Zechariah, chapter 9 and verse 9. 'Rejoice greatly … Shout, Daughter of Jerusalem! See your king comes to you, righteous and having salvation, gentle and riding on a donkey, on a colt, the foal of a donkey.' No prizes for knowing that's all about Jesus riding into Jerusalem at Easter time.

Now here's one for you to look up. Bible book Psalms, chapter 22 and verse 18 says 'They divide my garments among them and cast lots for my clothing.' Head for Bible book John, chapter 19 and verses 23 to 24 to find out if the advert came true.

43
SCAM-BUSH

Being a follower of Jesus can sometimes be a risky business, as a guy from the Bible (called Paul) knew only too well. Many of the Jewish religious leaders didn't like Paul talking about how Jesus was the Jewish Messiah (someone who God was gonna send to rescue them). Wherever Paul went, you could be sure that they'd roll up sooner or later to have a go at him.

In this Bible story (set in Jerusalem) the riled religious leaders managed to whip up such a frenzy against Paul that he was arrested by the Romans (who ruled the land) and taken away to be flogged. When the Roman commander discovered that Paul was a Roman citizen, he was promptly released. A head-to-head was arranged between the religious leaders and Paul to get to the bottom of what they were accusing him of. Smarty-pants Paul managed to get the religious leaders disagreeing with each other and a near riot broke out. Once again Paul was taken away to the soldiers' barracks, this time for his own safety.

Next day, forty of the disgruntled Jews swore not to eat another thing until Paul was killed. Paul's nephew soon got wind of the plot and made tracks to the army barracks

to spill the beans. Paul's enemies planned to ask the
Roman commander to bring Paul back to continue their
discussions, but only under the guise of ambushing
the poor chap and doing
away with him.

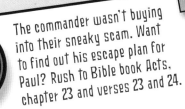

The commander wasn't buying
into their sneaky scam. Want
to find out his escape plan for
Paul? Rush to Bible book Acts,
chapter 23 and verses 23 and 24.

44

STAR TREK

Abram (later called Abraham) lived in Ur. His ancestors had settled there after coming off Noah's ark. Ur was a prosperous city and by all accounts Abram was a wealthy chap in his own right. Just when it looked like Abram could settle down to a nice, comfy life, his dad (Terah) decided to move the family to a place called Canaan (over 1,000 miles away!). Terah never actually made it that far. He stopped off along the way at Haran, where he eventually died.

When Abram was seventy-five years old, God turned up with a bit of news. He wanted Abram to up sticks and leave Haran and to head off in the direction of Canaan to finish the journey his dad had started. In those days you couldn't just hop on a plane and arrive at your destination a few hours later (cos planes hadn't been invented yet). There was nothing for it but to load up your camels and travel the hard way, by foot.

You're probably wondering why on earth God should ask an old man to make such a mahoosive journey, so I'll tell you. God was gonna start a brand-new nation of people who worshipped Him and who would gradually get to know Him. Abram was God's main man to get it all up and

running, and is one of the stars of the Bible. But first the
nation needed a bit of land to call their own, and that's
what Canaan was going to be. Just in case you were worried
that he'd get lonely all on his lonesome, let me put your
mind at rest. Abram also took with him his wife Sarai, his
nephew Lot and all his possessions and servants.

Arriving at Canaan wasn't like when you move to a new
house and it's empty. Canaan
still had people living
there. What was
Abram to do?

Had God made a mistake?
Have a read of Bible book
Genesis, chapter 12 and
verses 6 and 7 to find out.

45
RUNAWAY RELATIVE

Looking after his uncle Laban's flocks had been hard work and Jacob reckoned that he'd more than paid his way over the years. He'd acquired some sheep and goats of his own and now God had told him that it was high time he returned to the land of his birth (Canaan). To be honest, Laban's sons were cheesed off with Jacob and would be glad to see the back of him. They thought he'd done a bit too well out of their dad and was doing them out of what they reckoned was rightfully theirs. Jacob had a word with his wives Leah and Rachel on the quiet and filled them in on his plans to scarper.

While Laban and his sons were out in the fields, Jacob scrammed. Not only did he take his wives, his kids and his flocks, but that rascal Rachel ransacked her dad's place and nabbed his household gods (statues that he worshipped).

It wasn't until three days later that Laban found out his nephew and his daughters had run off. With his family in tow, Laban set off to catch Jacob. Seven days later he caught up with Jacob and his entourage. Before Laban had a chance to go steaming in, God appeared to him in a dream and

warned him to be careful what he said to Jacob (or he'd be in trouble).

Jacob tried to explain his side of the story to Laban and how he was worried that his uncle wouldn't let his wives go with him. For his part Laban said he just wanted to say one last goodbye to his daughters and his grandchildren – was that too much to ask? Oh, and by the way, who nicked his household gods? Jacob hadn't a clue, which was the truth. Finally he gave up the search and Jacob and his uncle decided to call a truce.

At daybreak the next day the men parted company.

Want to know what became of those elusive household gods? All will be revealed in Bible book Genesis, chapter 31 and verse 34.

JADED JONAH

Sometimes, when God has a message for someone, He sends one of His prophets to be the delivery boy. Jonah was one such chap, and God had told him to head off to Nineveh (in Assyria) to warn its inhabitants that God was calling time on their wicked ways. Unless they stopped being such rotters God was gonna wipe them off the face of the earth, or words to that effect. The Assyrians were arch enemies of Jonah's nation, and what a nasty bunch they were. You sure wouldn't want to mess with them. No siree! Jonah tried to head off in the opposite direction but God was having none of it. He pointed His prophet back in the direction of Nineveh and commanded Jonah to go and finish the job. Jonah reluctantly rocked up in Assyria's capital city and walked from one end of it to the other telling people that God was gonna destroy the place in forty days' time. Bet he was popular!

Nineveh was so big it took Jonah three days to complete his task. Now, here's the wild thing ... When the king of Nineveh got wind of God's warning he was mortified. He immediately sent out an order that no one was to eat anything (including the animals) and everyone was to humbly pray to God for His forgiveness for being such a bad bunch.

Because God is kind and fair, He changed His mind about punishing Nineveh. How good is that? Well, not according to Jonah. He went into a bit of a sulk that his wicked enemies hadn't copped it. God had a lesson He needed to teach jaded Jonah, so while the prophet rested for a bit, God made a plant grow up to shelter him from the heat of the sun. Early the next morning God destroyed the plant and sent a strong wind to pile on the heat. In no time at all Jonah was roasting in the scorching sun and wishing he were dead.

Want to find out what the lesson that God taught Jonah was? Head for Bible book Jonah, chapter 4 and verses 9 through to 11.

GLORY STORY

Being the leader of the Israelites was a toughie, and Moses needed all the help God could give him. The Israelites' job was to show the rest of the world what God was like, so it was mega important that they knew what He was like and that God was involved in everything they did. That's just how God wanted things to be. God wanted the Israelites to rely on Him and to trust Him. As for God and Moses, well, they got on like a house on fire and God bent over backwards to do most things Moses asked. Wow! How good is that?

So, when Moses popped the question that, if it was OK with God, could he see Him in all His brill glory and greatness, pretty please, God said yes. Well, sort of yes.

God told Moses to go and stand on a nearby rock and then wait. Sure enough, God appeared but, first off, He lifted Moses up, plonked him down in a crack in one of the rocks and covered him with His hand. Next up, God swept past Moses in all His awesome brilliance and then took His hand away so that Moses could see Him as He made His exit.

Want to know why God wouldn't let Moses see Him face to face? Head for Bible book Exodus, chapter 33 and verse 20.

48
OH NO, IT'S JOE!

Things were getting tough in the land of Canaan. A famine had hit the region and people were getting a bit desperate. The family of an old man called Jacob headed off to find food in Egypt. The governor of Egypt was none other than their long lost brother Joseph, who they'd sold as a slave many years earlier. They might not have recognised him but he sure knew who they were.

Joseph accused the brothers of being spies and had them thrown into jail. They protested their innocence, so Joseph let them prove it by going to fetch their youngest brother. He'd keep one of them (Simeon) banged up until they returned. That way Joseph told them he'd know if they were telling the truth. Was Joe giving them a hard time for nearly killing him all those years ago? Who knows, but whatever he was up to, Joseph was not finding it easy seeing his brothers again after all this time.

Joseph packed off the brothers with food, and when they arrived back in Canaan, Jacob was in two minds about letting them go back with Benjamin (his youngest son). He'd lost Joseph long ago, Simeon was locked up and what if Benjamin never came back. Eventually Jacob gave in. He

had nothing to lose. If they didn't get help soon they'd all starve anyway.

Back in Egypt, the brothers had to face Joseph once more. Joseph wanted to test his brothers to see if they were sorry for what they'd done to him all those years ago. When he finally realised that they were, he decided to tell them who he really was. It was tears all round. Everyone was blubbing and hugging each other and letting bygones be bygones.

The icing on the cake to this happy ending will bring a tear to your eye as well.

This tearjerker can be found in Bible book Genesis, chapter 46 and verses 28 to 30.

49
RAHAB RISKS IT

As we dive into this Bible story, Joshua has just gone and landed himself the juicy job of heading up the Israelite nation. The Israelites are about to conquer the land of Canaan and top of Joshua's 'to do' list is to send a couple of spies to find out what they're up against. Off they go to do their stuff, paying special attention to the city of Jericho, which Joshua planned to pummel first.

Once in the city, the covert couple took cover in the house of a prostitute (Rahab). Rahab knew which side her bread was buttered and quickly allied herself to the Israelites. Stories were flying around about how God had parted the Red Sea to rescue the Israelites from Egypt and of their victories in battle. The inhabitants of Jericho were wetting themselves worrying that they'd be next on Israel's hit list.

It looks like Joshua's two men weren't quite as good at this spying lark as they were cracked up to be cos word soon got out that they were holed up in Rahab's place. The king of Jericho sent a message to Rahab to hand over the spies or else, but the plucky lady hid them on the roof and fibbed that the spies had gone.

While the king's men headed off on a wild-goose chase to

track the spies down, Rahab helped the pair escape out of her window on a rope. Before they fled to the hills, Rahab made them promise that when the Israelites eventually came to attack her city, she and her family would be protected because of her good deed.

Did the spies agree to her request? Check out Bible book Joshua, chapter 2 and verses 17 through to 21.

MEGA MATES

Saul's days were numbered as Israel's king, but he wasn't too keen on the young fella (David) who God had lined up to replace him. To be honest, King Saul wanted David dead. To complicate matters, Saul's son (Jonathan) and David were best buddies.

The king had already used David for target practice and tried to kill him with a spear, and so Israel's king-in-waiting wasn't taking any more chances. He had a chat with Jonathan to find out whether Saul was still hopping mad at him. Jonathan knew nothing of any plots his dad might have to do away with David, but the pals agreed to put Saul to the test. David was meant to be at a dinner party with Saul but he wasn't gonna show up. The plan was that if his dad got angry about David being absent, Jonathan would say he'd gone to his home town for a special family occasion. As it was, Saul didn't say a word.

Next night, when once again David didn't appear, the king wasn't quite as calm as a cucumber as he'd been the day before. Actually he was spitting mad, and not only with David. Saul accused his son of taking sides with David and warned Jonathan that if that interloper David wasn't done

away with, Jonathan would never be king. Jonathan knew that already. He understood that David was God's choice and that was all that mattered.

The king was now so angry he even had a go at spearing his own son. Jonathan did a runner and went to warn David that his dad was on the warpath. He went outside, near to where David had been hiding and fired an arrow into the air. Jonathan had brought along a young lad with him to fetch the arrows. 'Isn't the arrow beyond you?' he shouted to the lad. That was the prearranged signal to David that it wasn't safe for him to stick around a moment longer. The best buddies made a peace pact with each other (and their descendants) and then went their separate ways.

Want to find out if David was as good as his word? Check it out in Bible book 2 Samuel, chapter 9 and verses 1 through to 7.

NATIONAL DISTRIBUTORS

UK: (and countries not listed below)
CWR, Waverley Abbey House, Waverley Lane, Farnham, Surrey GU9 8EP.
Tel: (01252) 784700 Outside UK (44) 1252 784700 Email: mail@cwr.org.uk

AUSTRALIA: KI Entertainment, Unit 21 317-321 Woodpark Road, Smithfield,
New South Wales 2164. Tel: 1 800 850 777 Fax: 02 9604 3699
Email: sales@kientertainment.com.au

CANADA: David C Cook Distribution Canada, PO Box 98, 55 Woodslee Avenue,
Paris, Ontario N3L 3E5. Tel: 1800 263 2664 Email: sandi.swanson@davidccook.ca

GHANA: Challenge Enterprises of Ghana, PO Box 5723, Accra.
Tel: (021) 222437/223249 Fax: (021) 226227 Email: ceg@africaonline.com.gh

HONG KONG: Cross Communications Ltd, 1/F, 562A Nathan Road, Kowloon.
Tel: 2780 1188 Fax: 2770 6229 Email: cross@crosshk.com

INDIA: Crystal Communications, 10-3-18/4/1, East Marredpalli, Secunderabad –
500026, Andhra Pradesh. Tel/Fax: (040) 27737145
Email: crystal_edwj@rediffmail.com

KENYA: Keswick Books and Gifts Ltd, PO Box 10242-00400, Nairobi.
Tel: (020) 2226047/312639 Email: sales.keswick@africaonline.co.ke

MALAYSIA: Canaanland, No. 25 Jalan PJU 1A/41B, NZX Commercial Centre,
Ara Jaya, 47301 Petaling Jaya, Selangor. Tel: (03) 7885 0540/1/2 Fax: (03) 7885 0545
Email: info@canaanland.com.my

Salvation Publishing & Distribution Sdn Bhd, 23 Jalan SS 2/64, 47300 Petaling Jaya,
Selangor. Tel: (03) 78766411/78766797 Fax: (03) 78757066/78756360
Email: info@salvationbookcentre.com

NEW ZEALAND: KI Entertainment, Unit 21 317-321 Woodpark Road, Smithfield,
New South Wales 2164, Australia. Tel: 0 800 850 777 Fax: +612 9604 3699
Email: sales@kientertainment.com.au

NIGERIA: FBFM, Helen Baugh House, 96 St Finbarr's College Road, Akoka, Lagos.
Tel: (01) 7747429/4700218/825775/827264 Email: fbfm_1@yahoo.com

PHILIPPINES: OMF Literature Inc, 776 Boni Avenue, Mandaluyong City.
Tel: (02) 531 2183 Fax: (02) 531 1960 Email: gloadlaon@omflit.com

SINGAPORE: Alby Commercial Enterprises Pte Ltd, 95 Kallang Avenue #04-00,
AIS Industrial Building, 339420. Tel: (65) 629 27238 Fax: (65) 629 27235
Email: marketing@alby.com.sg

SOUTH AFRICA: Struik Christian Books, 1st Floor, Wembley Square II,
§Solan Street, Gardens, Cape Town 8001, South Africa. Tel: (021) 460 5400
Fax: (021) 461 7662 Email: info@struikchristianmedia.co.za

SRI LANKA: Christombu Publications (Pvt) Ltd, Bartleet House, 65 Braybrooke
Place, Colombo 2. Tel: (9411) 2421073/2447665 Email: dhanad@bartleet.com

USA: David C Cook Distribution Canada, PO Box 98, 55 Woodslee Avenue, Paris,
Ontario N3L 3E5, Canada. Tel: 1800 263 2664 Email: sandi.swanson@davidccook.ca

CWR is a Registered Charity – Number 294387
CWR is a Limited Company registered in England – Registration Number 1990308

More of Andy Robb's colourful Bible stories with crazy cartoons and cliff-hanger endings, to stop you getting bored!

50 Goriest Bible Stories

A sword plunged to the hilt into a super-fat king's blubber, a bloke getting killed by lightning, cold-blooded murder, tons of people drowning, scary skin diseases, famines, earthquakes! Ready to be grossed out? Jump in!

ISBN: 978-1-85345-530-8

50 Weirdest Bible Stories

Discover fifty of the weirdest things that happened in the Bible including the crossing of the Red Sea, Jesus healing a paralysed man, heavenly bread in the desert, the strange dreams of Joseph, Peter walking on water and many more. Want some weirdness? Go for it!

ISBN: 978-1-85345-489-9

50 Craziest Bible Stories

Some crazy things happened in the Bible like the stories of Jonah and the big fish, Elijah and the prophets of Baal, Balaam and the donkey, the feeding of the 5,000, and Jesus' resurrection. Go on – get ka-rayzee!

ISBN: 978-1-85345-490-5

50 Barmiest Bible Stories

Among the collection are the stories of how the universe kicked off; how the Israelites escaped from Egypt and spent forty years grumbling in the desert; how Jesus was God's chosen man to sort out the mess humankind had made of the world; and what the good and bad kings of Israel got up to.

ISBN: 978-1-85345-852-1

50 Jammiest Bible Stories

A boy who attended his own funeral, a man who lived to be an eye-boggling 930 years old, a duo of jail-breakers who got away with it ... The Bible tells us about some remarkable events, and this book will help to introduce readers to the equally remarkable God who lies behind those events.

ISBN: 978-1-85345-851-4

For current prices visit **www.cwr.org.uk**
Available online or from Christian bookshops.

MORE FROM ANDY ROBB

Professor Bumblebrain offers some exciting explanations, colourful cartoons and (ahem) 'hilarious' jokes answering these important questions:

Who is God? What is He like?
Where does He live?
How can I get to know Him?
ISBN: 978-1-85345-579-7

Who's the bravest? Who's the
funniest? Who's the jammiest?
Who's the strongest?
ISBN: 978-1-85345-578-0

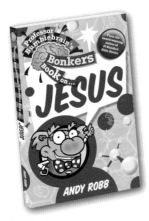

Who is Jesus? Where did He come
from? What was His mission?
What's it to me?
ISBN: 978-1-85345-623-7

Who made the universe? How old is
planet earth? What about dinosaurs?
Was there really a worldwide flood?
ISBN: 978-1-85345-622-0

For current prices visit **www.cwr.org.uk**
Available online or from Christian bookshops.

Get into God's Word

Topz is a popular bimonthly devotional for 7- to 11-year-olds.

The Topz Gang teach children biblical truths through daily Bible readings, word games, puzzles, riddles, cartoons, competitions and simple prayers.

Only **£2.85** each
or **£15.50** (UK) for a year's subscription (six issues)

YP's is a dynamic bimonthly devotional for 11- to 15-year-olds.

Each issue is packed with cool graphics, special features and articles, plus daily Bible readings and notes for two months.

Only **£2.85** each
or **£15.50** (UK) for a year's subscription (six issues)

Prices correct at time of printing
Available online or from Christian bookshops.

Danny's Daring Days

Talented footballer Danny learns how to step out in faith, believing that God and His love will always be with him.

ISBN: 978-1-85345-502-5

John's Jam-Packed Jottings

John learns about loyalty to Jesus and God's forgiving nature.

ISBN: 978-1-85345-503-2

Josie's Jazzy Journal

Josie, with the help of best friend Sarah, learns how to show God's love.

ISBN: 978-1-85345-457-8

Paul's Potty Pages

Paul from the Topz Gang tries to impress the new American girl in his class, with disastrous results!

ISBN: 978-1-85345-456-1

Benny's Barmy Bits

Discover with Benny how God wants to be the most important part of our lives.

ISBN: 978-1-85345-431-8

Sarah's Secret Scribblings

Join Sarah from the Topz Gang as she learns to pray for people who upset her, discovers that everyone is special to God, and more.

ISBN: 978-1-85345-432-5

Dave's Dizzy Doodles

Dave discovers it's never too late for God to turn things around.

ISBN: 978-1-85345-552-0

Gruff & Saucy's Topzy-Turvy Tales

Gruff and Saucy learn that, although it's sometimes hard trying to live God's way, He gives us the Holy Spirit to help us.

ISBN: 978-1-85345-553-7

These special editions of *Topz Secret Diaries* will help you discover things about yourself and God with questions and quizzes, puzzles, word searches, doodles, lists to write and more.

Topz Secret Diaries: Boys Only

ISBN: 978-1-85345-596-4

Topz Secret Diaries: Just for Girls

ISBN: 978-1-85345-597-1

For current prices visit **www.cwr.org.uk**
Available online or from Christian bookshops.